LUCID
TRAVELER

To my aunt Claudia,

Though you're no longer with us,
I still get to see you in my dreams

Editing: Krysten Garcia

Book Design and Typesetting: Ashlyn Lance

First Edition. Paperback.

EPUB ISBN: 979-8-9869850-3-9

Paperback ISBN: 979-8-9869850-4-6

www.ashlynlance.com

WELCOME

TRAVELER

You spend one-third of your life asleep and a fraction of that in your dreams, so why not take the reigns and awaken the conscious dreamer within?

Most people 'go through the motions' of their dreams, never giving them another thought, but *you* don't. There are many like yourself who are eager to take control of their dreams, and there are even more of us who've already begun to master it.

In this guide, all the magic is broken down into practical steps to demystify this ancient practice, and with some time, you'll effortlessly step into your dream world whenever you want.

Become a
Lucid Traveler.

The Author's Journey

My dreaming journey began in my early years, when I would regularly wake up in the middle of the night for no reason. Little did I know that my natural circadian rhythm matched perfectly with one of the lucid dreaming induction techniques known as Wake-Back-to-Bed. This led to many nights where I would find myself desperately trying to break free of my recurring sleep paralysis.

And one day, I did manage to break free, and I violently crashed onto the floor below, jolting me awake. To my surprise, I saw that I was still neatly tucked into bed as if I had never moved. Feeling the crash, the rolling—everything—it was so vivid as if I had actually done it—but I hadn't, and I couldn't explain it. This night is the night that started me down the path of dream magic.

Lucid dreams would happen every so often after that, and I wrongly believed they were just random occurrences. That is until I gave birth to my first child. When you care for a newborn, you get stretches of about three to five hours of sleep—a schedule that I'm familiar with—and in those sleep deprived days, I would lucid dream almost daily. That's when the connection clicked. The same frequency of lucid dreams happened again when I had my second child, but by that time, my dream world was easily navigable. As my children grew and required less sleep, I would take afternoon naps, another confirmed entry point for lucid dreaming.

Almost a decade later, it's my wish to share this ability with those who are willing to give it a try.

Don't live a life without it.

How to be a lucid traveler

Drifting away
Sleep
Dreams
Lucid Dreams

Realization

Reality checks
Dream Recall
Brainwave Entrainment
Meditation
Herbs
Intention setting

Emerging Lucid

Ascend

Morning

While some individuals have a natural talent for lucid dreaming, it's still a skill, and like all skills, it takes time and dedication to develop. You, too, can take part in the incredible experience of consciously controlling your dreams by sticking to a routine.

> Reaching lucidity is a highly transformative experience. The rewards that come with it are more than worth the effort.

Always Have an Open Mind

Why do you want to pursue this ability? Take a
moment to think. Your answer will help your
motivation last despite setbacks.

Consistency

It may take some time before first reaching lucidity,
but you'll soon have that dream that changes
everything. After that, you'll never want to stop.

The Power of You

Believe in your ability to learn and control your
dreams. Positive affirmations and thoughts can
only help you.

Finding Community

Find friends with similar interests or
consider sharing this book with
someone you know.

Throughout the ages, dreams have held a mysterious sway over humanity, quietly influencing us from our subconscious. Artists, writers, inventors, and more have all drawn inspiration from their dreams. Many ancient cultures also understood the power of dreams—some were adept at lucid dreaming, others turned to dream divination for guidance.

These ancient traditions laid the groundwork for the modern exploration of the dream state, where it has become a well-documented and scientifically studied phenomenon. Dreamers in a lucid state are able to move their eyes on command, signaling to researchers that they are conscious and aware despite being fast asleep. This research enables highly lucid individuals to participate in experimental research to further study this amazing ability.

DRIFTING AWAY

Sleep

The process of sleep is broken down into sleep cycles. There are four stages in a cycle, each with a distinct part to play in your overall well-being. The first three stages are the 'Non-Rapid Eye Movement' phase, known as 'NREM', and the fourth stage is Rapid Eye Movement or 'REM'. A complete cycle lasts about ninety minutes and continually repeats throughout the night, with each episode of the 'NREM' periods getting shorter and shorter. This increases the time spent in REM sleep, priming your early morning hours for vivid and intense dreams.

N1

The first stage in the sleep cycle is known as 'N1'. Consider this a transitional phase where your mind begins taking you across the bridge from reality to your inner dream world. You experience intense drowsiness and a sense of drifting in and out of consciousness. Hypnagogia is also a common occurrence in this stage —unusual sensations and fleeting dream-like imagery tend to appear. It's thought that Hypnagogia occurs from the brain blending elements of the real world and your dreams. N1 is also when you experience hypnagogic jerks, where your muscles suddenly contract, startling you awake.

N2

The next stage is known as Light Sleep or as 'N2', and it makes up about fifty percent of the sleep cycle. Essential for overall sleep quality, this period is when you completely disconnect from reality and show all the typical characteristics of sleep. This stage helps with memory consolidation and processing

N3

The 'N3' stage is Slow-wave Sleep or Deep Sleep. Twenty-five percent of the sleep cycle is dedicated to this stage. This phase releases hormones that kickstart our body's healing processes. Your immune system is reinforced, supporting your ability to fend off sickness. At the same time, your tissues, muscles, and bones begin repairing, making 'N3' essential for recovery.

N4

The final stage of the sleep cycle, known as 'REM' or Rapid Eye Movement, is characterized by heightened brain activity resembling wakefulness and darting eye movements. Your muscles also lock into sleep paralysis, which prevents you from physically acting out your dreams.

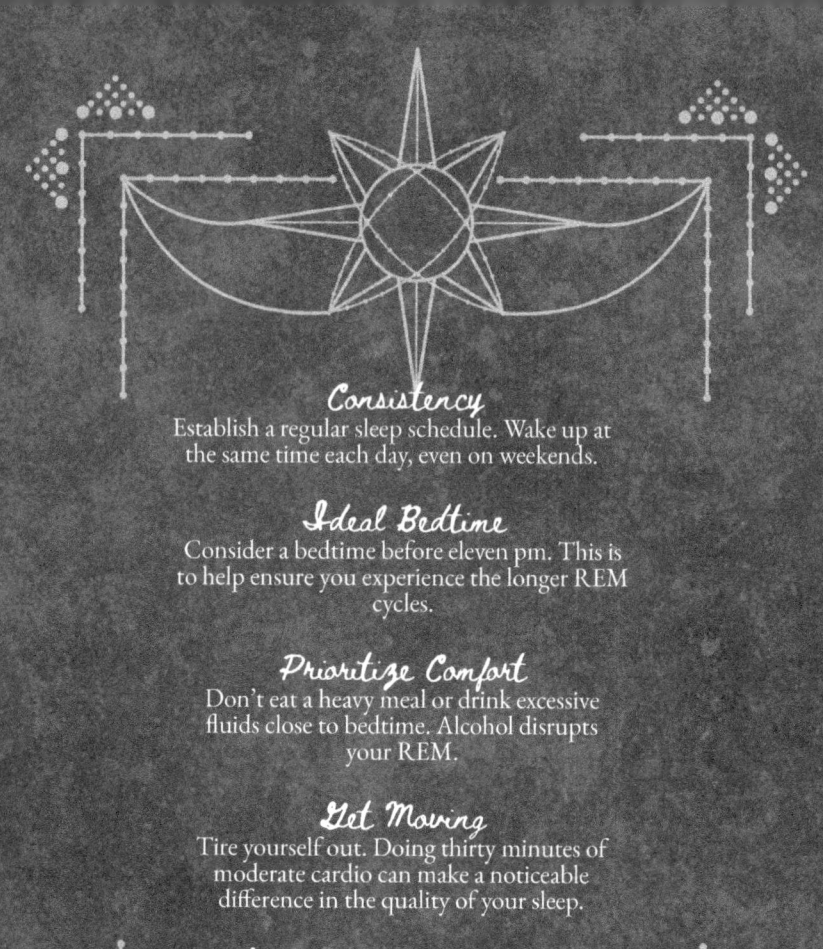

Consistency

Establish a regular sleep schedule. Wake up at the same time each day, even on weekends.

Ideal Bedtime

Consider a bedtime before eleven pm. This is to help ensure you experience the longer REM cycles.

Prioritize Comfort

Don't eat a heavy meal or drink excessive fluids close to bedtime. Alcohol disrupts your REM.

Get Moving

Tire yourself out. Doing thirty minutes of moderate cardio can make a noticeable difference in the quality of your sleep.

Early Morning Sunlight

Exposure to morning sunlight regulates your internal clock, reinforcing wakefulness throughout the day

Sleep is the way into your dreams.

Make it good.

Dreams

As an avid dreamer, it seems strange that dreams are glossed over in waking life. At best they're misunderstood. At worst they're brushed off as irrelevant nonsense, best left to be forgotten and discarded.

Due to certain connotations formed in the modern era, dreams have become more synonymous with 'a wish for something' more than anything else. While dreams are a great source of inspiration, they're just a creative tool—not a replacement for work done in the real world. Your dreams can't alter your reality, but they're more than capable of transcending it.

We dismiss the ways dreams affect us, waving them away as if they have little to no impact on your well-being. Whether or not you remember them, the energy they leave you with can impact the rest of your day, for good or bad.

Consider nightmares. They're portrayed as unescapable prisons. When you wake up from one, how long does it take to shake off the fear? If they're left to be forgotten because 'it was just a dream', you risk letting trauma fester. These types of dreams are representations of your negative emotions and should be examined to get a deeper understanding of their cause.

There's a reason for nightmares, and it's not to haunt or hurt you. It's a sign to work through your issues. Lucid dreaming, when used for self-actualization, begins this process of healing.

So dreams are either ineffective tools of manifestation or harbingers of fear. It's no wonder why lucid dreaming isn't widely practiced in current times. We, as a society, have very little understanding of dreaming in general. Some believe that dreams are just a protective mechanism to keep our brains running. Others believe that dreaming allows you to decompress the day safely. Either way, understanding the mechanics is unnecessary for reaching lucidity.

It goes something like this: While you're awake, your brain processes sensory input, creating the reality you perceive. Everything you've ever experienced comes from here, the real world. As you wind down and relax, you might start to daydream a bit, slipping into dream-like imagery, and then you fall asleep. You lose consciousness and wake up hours later with no recollection of the hours that passed. So the question is, if all of your sensory input from the real world has shut down, how is your mind able to create an immersive world that has all the potential to rival waking life? You can see, hear, feel, taste, and think just the same, yet you're unconscious. What happens during sleep that allows this? We may never know.

What we do know is that your dream world is anchored by the memories of the real world—all your thoughts, emotions, beliefs, surroundings, your day, and even the media you consume influence your subconscious. You live in a reality that exists and continues on independently of you.

Your dreams, on the other hand, lack that external force. Your dream world exists and operates beyond the constraints of reality—beyond the constraints of known science even—and is limited only by the strength of your imaginative powers.

Lucid Dreaming

We've been conditioned to believe we have no control over our dreams. We've never learned as a collective that dreams are an extremely powerful tool of introspection, but even with all the forces working against your empowerment, it's never been easier to break free of these false beliefs. All it takes is a single conscious thought:

Am I dreaming?

Lucidity is nothing more than an altered state of awareness. It's when you manage to 'wake up' in your dream world and regain the use of your conscious thoughts and senses while still asleep.

How does this book feel in your hands? How warm are you? What sounds do you hear happening around you? This conscious awareness is your gateway out of being an unconscious dreamer.

People don't usually question reality, let alone their dreams. When starting out, you won't feel the instinct to question whether or not you're dreaming either. This is why the phrase "Am I dreaming?" or any other derivative of it is so crucial. By rewiring your thought processes to automatically question yourself, you'll remember to ask while still in a dream. Replying in any way will usually free you from the predetermined dream narrative. You'll then regain conscious awareness and have the power to control your dream with nothing but your thoughts.

Becoming lucid may seem like an impossible feat to the uninitiated, but it's only the beginning. Those with mastery are even more impressive, controlling their entire dreamscape. Money is of no object. The rules of the natural worlds? Irrelevant. There's a level of creativity that can't ever be experienced anywhere else. You can also confront and resolve emotional wounds, analyze problems from a new perspective, or even safely take part in life-threatening activities.

One of my go-to experiences is free falling through the sky. The rushing wind, my stomach knotting, the weightlessness of it all—yes, it feels so terrifyingly real! Have an important event or performance coming up? Take advantage of the time distortion and squeeze in a few hours of practice in seconds. I would sprint through red-rock mountains in my dreams, and although it didn't translate into running faster in real life, it did provide me with the physical sensation of going top-speed, becoming a gauge of just how much improvement I really needed.

REALIZATION

Reality Checks

Ask yourself right now, are you dreaming? How sure of that are you? Reality checks are simple gestures with predictable results which prove to yourself whether or not you're dreaming. Questioning your reality, no matter how briefly, is the secret to success. Their effectiveness is directly reliant on how well you play the skeptic. If you absent-mindedly do a reality check, you'll never stop to realize whether or not you're actually dreaming. Without a method of conscious awareness attached, reality checks will become nothing more than learned behaviors on autopilot. Always pair reality checks with "Am I dreaming?" or "Is this a dream?"

Push your finger through your palm

> Your finger will pass through effortlessly in a dream.

Count your fingers

> The number of fingers you have might change or look weird.

Read a passage of text twice

> You may only need to read it once to see gibberish or nonsensical words.

Check a clock

> Glance, look away, then check again. They'll never be the same twice in a dream.

Do a double take of yourself in a mirror

> You won't look the same, or the mirror will show something else.

Jump up and down

>Gravity won't affect you in the same way.

Hold your nose shut and try to breathe

>If you can still breathe, then you're dreaming.

Check your reflection in water

>Like mirrors, almost all reflections are distorted.

Recall how you arrived

>Don't remember? You might be dreaming.

Listen to background noise

>Do you hear whatever you're expecting to? If not, consider what you should be hearing.

Check your phone or computer

>It won't work the same if you're in a dream.

Ask yourself again if you're dreaming, this time doing a reality check. Was everything as you expected it to be? They're also useful once you're lucid, acting as a double confirmation that you're in your dream world.

Dream Recall

To succeed in lucid dreaming, it's essential that you remember your dreams. We usually experience between three to five dreams throughout the night, but because of memory suppressing hormones released during early sleep cycles, we remember very little. There can be no progress without strong dream recall. Having a lucid dream and forgetting is extremely likely otherwise. For this reason, a dream journal is a must.

Your best chances of remembering are during the first few moments of wakefulness or when you're still groggy. Stay absolutely still and avoid thoughts other then the ones you've just dreamed of. Don't hesitate. Dreams tend to fade quickly. Attempt to reconstruct whatever you remember down to the finest little details.

Writing down your dream rather than recording it by voice is preferred, but if there's no way you can write, then speaking it aloud is better than forgoing it altogether. Use keywords, drawings, emotions, or anything else that'll help you connect with your dreams. Even if you only recall fragments, record everything you can. How did the dream make you feel? Who did it made you think about?

There are apps designed to assist with lucid dreaming, offering features like dream journals, reality check reminders, and sleep tracking. This is the easiest way to stay on track with journaling.

If it seems too complicated, start out with the most important parts of the dream and work from there. If you miss this window, there's another chance to remember once you're in bed again—you might get lucky and get flashbacks, giving you a second chance to record it. Aim to remember at least one or two dreams every night and work further by remembering three.

When you begin filling your dream journal, you'll start to see some patterns emerging. Whatever tends to show up again and again is considered a dream sign. Dream signs can be characters, emotions, events, or even locations. Create a separate list of these in the back of your journal to catalog for future use.

Maybe you always find yourself walking on the ceiling or watching a purple sunset? Have dreams of betrayal? Dreams of war? Ever had a talking animal companion accompany you? Or maybe you always come across someone who you never remember meeting? You'll begin to notice these signs as they play out time and time again, leading you to eventually recognize them while in a dream, triggering lucidity.

Brainwave Entrainment

Binaural Beats, Isochronic Tones, and Singing Bowl frequencies are all forms of Brainwave Entrainment, a phenomenon where your brainwaves naturally synchronize with external forces. Brainwave entrainment has gained much popularity over the years due to it's potential therapeutic and meditative benefits by inducing brainwaves states simply by listening.

Gamma (100-30 Hz)	Advanced learning. Mental agility. Innovative thinking. Enhanced sensory perception.
Beta (30-13 Hz)	Alert. Focused. Work productivity. Social Interactions. Stressful situations. Achievement mindset.
Alpha (13-8 Hz)	Calm mental state. Stress reduction. Creative inspiration. Light meditation. Enhanced intuition. Emotional stability.
Theta (8-4 Hz)	Deep meditation. Dream-like state. Emotional healing. Expanded consciousness. Hypnagogic state.
Delta (4-0.5Hz)	Deep Sleep. Anti-aging. Healing and recovery. Regeneration. Immune system support.

Binaural Beats utilize the "frequency following response" where two different audio frequencies play in each ear. The difference in Hz levels is the brainwave you actually experience. For example, if one ear hears 300 Hz and the other hears 310Hz, then the tone your brain actually hears is 10 Hz, putting you in an Alpha State. Stereo headphones are mandatory for this reason.

Isochronic tones are audio pulses already set to a specific frequency. They don't require headphones since they're effective played through a single channel.

Singing bowls are traditional instruments made of metal or crystal. When struck by a mallet, these tuned bowls resonate a resoundingly smooth frequency, influencing your mental state. They're believed to have healing properties and promote a sense of well-being.

These auditory aids are highly accessible and are found on many streaming platforms at no extra cost. Simply type (a brainwave state) + (singing bowl frequency, binaural beat, or isochronic tone) on a search bar and thousands of options will appear. Experiment with listening to these as needed.

Meditation

Meditation is a great tool to enhance your visualization skills. These exercises will have you working on sculpting detailed reproductions of the real world like a mental workout. Dreams are built in your mind but it's your imagination that drives it.

Relax in a comfortable position, laying or sitting. Close your eyes. Allow your attention to come to your breath, observing your natural rhythm as you inhale and exhale. Let your thoughts come and go, but keep your focus on your breath until you feel absolute relaxation. This calmness is your brain shifting into an alpha or theta state. It can take anywhere from five to forty-five minutes for you to get to this point. If you find your mind is cluttered, taking very deep breaths from your belly may help. Be sure to expand your midsection as far out as you can to get the full effect.

Level One

Delve into the spectrum of colors. Consider the emotions or memories they bring up and cycle through as many as you can. Vary the level of intensity and saturation like a color picker.

Level Two

Create intricate multi-sensory models of objects. For example, think of strawberry—remember the feel of its pitted, seeded skin and its crisp, velvety leaves. Taste the strawberry on your tongue. As you progress, be sure to challenge yourself with more and more complex objects to construct.

Level Three

Recreate a setting from your everyday life. Build layers upon layers of details, walking yourself into the vision. Tune into any ambient sounds you'd normally be surrounded by in this place. Wind howling in your ear? Birds chirping? Vividly feel textures against your skin. Is there grass beneath your feet? Sand between your toes? Continue building this scene until you feel physically present in that space. Try to immerse yourself to the point where you can almost believe that you've been transported away.

Herbs

Certain herbs are believed to be beneficial for activating and assisting with lucid dreaming. Some can intensify your dreams, others may help you recognize the fact that you're dreaming. Most herbs generally used for anti-anxiety, sleep, memory, and stress relief seem to be useful to include as additional lucid dreaming support. Here are a few examples of herbs with their generally recognized folk medicine usage.

Blue Lotus

Ancient Egyptians used this euphoric herb as an aphrodisiac.

Calea Zacatechichi

Used throughout pre-Columbian Mexico for dream induction.

California Poppy

This herb has sedative, antidepressant, and calming properties.

Catnip

An old sleep aid known since roman times.

Ginkgo Biloba

An herb that helps with all things relating to memory.

Lavender

This herb is known for reducing anxiety, insomnia, and restlessness.

Lemon Balm

Is a stress-reliever, a sleep inducer, and nervous system regulator.

Mugwort

This potent herb intensifies dreams and helps with dream recall.

Shatavari

Known to increase the vividness of dreams.

Valerian Root

This herb was used as a sedative during medieval times.

Vervain

Has relaxant and anti-anxiety properties.

Intention Setting

Unlocking the potential of lucid dreaming involves understanding that your dream world is a manifestation of your own mind—a world built for you, by you. And while you are always in control, it may not feel that way initially.

The ripple effect of your dreams, whether or not you remember them, has considerable influence on you when you wake up. The happiness that follows after a beautiful dream can brighten the rest of your day. While on the other side, a nightmare can leave you feeling anxious or moody and ruin your day before its even starts. The emotional impact is even more potent when it comes to lucid dreaming.

A moment of weakness can inadvertently lead you into the darkest parts of your subconscious mind, frightening you to the point of never wanting to lucid dream again. Overcoming this fear should be one of your highest priorities. By establishing clear intentions in the beginning, you can help set the tone of the journey. Try repeating an affirmation to help you remember that you are always in complete control.

Start your day by recording every detail you
recall from your dreams. This not only
solidifies your fading dreams, but also provides
valuable reference for later.

Do reality checks multiple times per day.
Regularly question, "Am I dreaming?"

Find your dream signs in real life and fail reality
checks. Doing this reprograms your mind to
connect the action to the dream sign in the real
world and in your dream world.

Dedicate a few minutes to meditation, a
cornerstone in your journey to lucid dreaming,
and refine your mental creative abilities.

Seize idle moments to daydream, treating
it as a test run in your world-building
skills. Consider it a rehearsal.

Despite the life-changing nature of lucid dreaming, the investment of the time and effort to build the groundwork is surprisingly doable.

EMERGE LUCID

There are two periods of heightened mental and dream activity that offer huge advantages to lucid dreaming. Triple your chances of having a lucid dream by using these strategic windows alongside your usual bedtime.

Afternoon Naps

These are prime mental hours where your mind is naturally alert and much more capable of 'waking up' while still in a dream. This creates a naturally easier entry point into your dream world.

Dark Early Mornings

Waking during the window between four am and six am takes advantage of the longer REM cycles that are most conductive to lucid dreaming. Your dreaming power is much more potent at this time.

Dream Induced Lucid Dream

DILD

Dream Induced Lucid dream is an occurrence, not a method. DILD is when you spontaneously realize that you're dreaming while still in your dream world. Maybe you used a reality check and found that your finger *was* actually going through your palm. Maybe your suspicion of reality finally kicked in, and you found yourself asking, "Am I dreaming?" while still in a dream. This is a huge success and a sign that you've done enough work in your foundational training to trickle through to your subconscious.

Wake Back To Bed
WBTB

Wake-Back-to-Bed creates the perfect storm for lucid dreaming by interrupting your typical sleep pattern to exploit the long REM of later sleep cycles.

You set an alarm to wake up after five to six hours of initial sleep. Stay up for about fifteen to twenty minutes. Get a glass of water, stretch, or read a book—do whatever you can to not fall asleep. Don't use blue screen devices, or you risk staying awake. After the waking period ends, let yourself fall asleep as usual. This little break heightens your mental alertness as you sleep, and it'll be much easier to remember you're dreaming.

WBTB is the perfect method for someone unable to develop a consistent practice due to lifestyle constraints. Your chances of randomly becoming lucid are significantly higher than your baseline.

Mnemonic Induction of Lucid Dream
MILD

The Mnemonic Induction of Lucid Dreams (MILD) technique is a popular approach developed by Dr. Stephen LaBerge. This method reinforces your intention to become lucid by creating strong associations between 'wanting to lucid dream' and falling asleep.

Before you drift off, shut your eyes and focus on a specific phrase, such as, "I'm in a dream" or "I'm dreaming." At the same time, visualize yourself encountering one of your dream signs and failing a reality check. This is intention implantation—this is you telling your mind that you want to have this experience in a dream. The more dream signs you can imagine running into, the better your chances of success will be. Continue with both the affirmations and 'failing reality check' imagery until you fall asleep naturally.

MILD takes advantage of the suggestibility of the hypnagogic state, where your thoughts are more likely to carry into your dreams. The phrase and imagery should begin to infiltrate your subconscious after a few nights, making it much easier to remember during future lucid dreaming attempts.

Wake Induced Lucid Dream
WILD

WILD is an approach that focuses on consciously bypassing NREM sleep. This method requires you to maintain just enough awareness as you enter REM to seamlessly transition to a lucid dream.

Close your eyes and maintain a state of deep relaxation. Think of counting, focus on breathing, or do anything that requires small amounts of mental effort while continuously telling yourself that you're dreaming. Your mind will then begin to test your body to see if its actually fallen asleep. You'll feel random urges to move, an undying need to swallow saliva, or have a need to scratch a phantom itch, but you have to resist. If you move for any reason, the test will fail, and you'll reset to NREM.

If you manage to pass all the checks, you'll then enter REM semi-awake. Reaching this point is highly personal and will vary between individuals and even days. No two dream entrances will be the same. You could see abstract shapes, hear phantom sounds, or even feel floating sensations. Acknowledge whatever you come across and continue on.

At this point, you should hear your own voice reminding you that you're dreaming and become fully lucid.

Senses Initiated Lucid Dream
SSILD

The Senses Initiated Lucid Dream (SSILD) technique was developed by lucid dreaming enthusiast, CosmicIron. SSILD is a straightforward approach which involves cycling through different senses to expand your self-awareness.

First, focus on the darkness of your closed eyes, making sure there is no strain or tension. Allow yourself to see whatever images come through. Next, you disengage your visual focus and turn your awareness onto sounds, internal or external. See if any voices or sounds manifest. Lastly, shift your awareness onto any physical sensations happening in your body. How does the blanket feel against your skin? Are there any drafts making you cold?

When you begin, you should spend only a few seconds on each sense, but as you grow more and more relaxed, lengthen the time slowly to eventually reach half a minute each.

Repeat this sense cycling and until you fall asleep.

'Crashing' into a Lucid Dream

This happens when I stay up so late that I can barely keep my eyes open. It's the same feeling you get when you really want to finish a movie, but you're so tired you don't even realize that you've already fallen asleep. It's essentially staying up for as long as you possibly can while struggling to remain awake. I repeatedly command myself to stay awake, and eventually, I'll 'crash' or pass out into a lucid dream. The results are immediate, but it always ruins my sleeping schedule.

'Escaping' to a Lucid Dream

Over the years, I've learned to recognize the moment when I enter the Hypnagogic State. It usually involves completely random imagery coupled with immediate amnesia of what I've just seen. When I enter this state, I remind myself that I'm dreaming and begin to forcefully "climb" out of my body, like a separation almost. I have to fight my way out, but by the end of the struggle, I'm standing in my bedroom. As I wander, all the same sensations of physically moving are present, yet I know I'm still asleep. When I discovered this technique, I wanted to know if I was inhabiting the real world or my dream world, so I did my own reality check and rearranged a few items like shoes, books, and paintings. When I woke up, it wasn't the mess I had made—everything had remained in their original positions. Despite feeling completely real, the space I explored was proven to be my dream world.

I f you've experienced any sort of conscious awareness
for any length of time, than congratulations, you've
gone lucid! If you're having trouble reaching lucidity
despite consistent practice, don't feel as if you've failed.
There's a lot of valuable experience that can help you in
your future attempts. Remember, you have an
opportunity to succeed every time you fall asleep, so
there's no need to rush yourself on this journey.

A magical experience like lucid dreaming is more than worthy of your dedication.

It's not a matter of if you will, it's a matter of when you will.

ASCEND THE DREAM

Stabilization

You've done the hardest part. You're in your dream world, conscious and aware, but now you face a new problem—controlling the stability of your dream. Lucidity is a delicate balance between emotion and restraint, and when the power of your dreams shifts into your hands, it's hard not to go wild. Except it's possible to lose it within seconds—even the realization that you've reached lucidity is enough to trigger a wake up.

Your dream world is inherently unstable. Control your breathing. Acknowledge that something exciting is happening, then let that feeling pass. As you gain experience, the initial excitement will be easier to control.

If you find yourself fully conscious in your dream world, but your dream is starting to fade away, activate your sense of touch to ground you. Touch anything and everything you can. It'll force your mind to fill in your dream world with detail, solidifying it.

Another known technique is dream-spinning, where you twirl around in place until your dream world is vivid and stable again. Feeding your body movement prevents you from waking up.

Staring down at your hands is another effective method of stabilization that has no real explanation for how or why it works. Alternatively, open and close your dream eyes.

Dream stabilization shouldn't be a big part of your process because even overthinking can catapult you back to bed. Only take a second or two to do these actions. They should work quickly.

So what's next?

Expecting your dream world to bend to your will immediately is unrealistic. In the beginning, you'll most likely only have the freedom of movement within an already set narrative, or maybe you'll only have decision-making capabilities. Full-on dream world creation is completely dependent on your level of focus and creative mental strength. It's not automatic. This is why mental exercises and practice are crucial for strengthening your creative power level. You're only as strong as your mind. When you finally break through the barrier, here are some ideas to get you started.

Experience super-human strength, fly through the sky or breath underwater.

Eat as much of your favorite food as you want.

Meet legends or mythical creatures, then explore and take part of their worlds.

Shape-shift into any animal or form you want and experience life as something other than a human.

Transport yourself to any time or era and converse with an important historical figure.

Fight in a colosseum battle against impossible odds.

Experience the rush of a free fall

Skill Improvement

Have you ever had a dream where you excelled at your hobbies or performances? These type of dreams switch on muscle activity just the same as their real-world counterparts do, but since you're in sleep paralysis as you dream, a different neural path is taken. This altered pathway lets you to fine tune your technique even better than if you were awake.

Refine your technique on a musical instrument or compose new music.

Play sports with your idols.

Overcome public speaking fears by addressing dream audiences.

Explore artistic creations in your dream and find inspiration that can't be found anywhere else.

Workout a real life problem using dream logic.

Play strategy games with your dream characters.

Perfect martial art forms or spar to better your technique and performance.

Healing

Lucid dreaming can be used to delve into the complex nature of your subconscious. You can easily face your inner thoughts, emotions, and memories as they come to surface. They can take on any form but are commonly represented as archetypal dream characters, beloved fictional characters, or familiar faces. You can better understand your mental state by interacting with them.

Relive past memories and rebuild them in a positive light.

**Stand in a blank space and command a door to appear before you.
Open it. Who comes out?**

Purposefully enter a nightmare to work on confronting your fears.

Learn to reframe anxieties or lessen their power over you.

Rewrite emotionally damaging mental scripts

Connect with your inner child. Explore the adventurous side of lucid dreaming.

Practice meditation and connect closely to higher guidance.

Approaching healing from your dream world provides a safe and immersive environment to see life from a new perspective.

You are in control.

What if my dream turns dark?

Nightmares are dreams that leave you waking in terror. They're much more powerful than a bad dream and often have a psychological component triggering them. These types of dreams thrive on your fear.

Never forget that you have absolute control over your dream world, even if it doesn't feel like it in the moment. By programming reality checks into your mind, you'll be able to reach lucidity and change the course of the dream narrative. Tell yourself that this dream isn't what you want to experience and shut it down—it really works. Also, closing your eyes and consciously choosing to wake up will end the dream.

Dreams have a natural time limit of about an hour. So have no fear. Realize that you can't be harmed in any way. You are always safe.

MORNING

If you face an untimely awakening, there's a very good chance you can return to REM and gain conscious entry into another lucid dream. Lay exceptionally still, as if you never woke up, then use your favorite lucid dreaming induction technique.

Hypnopompia

Hypnopompia is the other side of the half-conscious sleep bridge. You experience the same hallucinations, light shows, sounds, and sensations as hypnogogia, but now it happens as you wake up.

Sleep Paralysis

You can't scream, open your eyes, or even wake up, so what do you do? While experiencing sleep paralysis can be unpleasant, you can use this state to easily transition to a lucid dream. When you find yourself trapped, you have to learn to not fight it. Panicking will only make the experience last longer and take you away from your ultimate goal, lucidity.

If you find yourself coming undone, remind yourself that you'll be awake soon. Your body does this everyday. You just happen to be awake for it this time.

It's a doorway. All you have to do is step through it.

False Awakenings

False awakenings are probably one of the most frustrating experiences in lucid dreaming. You believe you've woken up from sleep, only to realize you're still in a dream. This usually chains into many, many awakenings, making you feel as if you're stuck in an endless loop. After four or five 'awakenings', it's easy to become desperate for the real world.

The solution to dealing with this is simple—forget trying to wake up and just enjoy being lucid for a while longer. It can become anxiety-inducing otherwise.

True awakening

Like all good things, lucid dreams, too, must come to an end. Challenge yourself have an "x" amount of lucid dreams a month and work on refining your creative abilities. Over time, your dream world will be under your total control.

With dedication and consistency, you won't have to practice reaching lucidity for the rest of your life. Once you understand and have successfully navigated a few lucid dreams, you'll be set for life.

This is only the beginning. You can only get stronger in your creative abilities. So, as you lay in bed at night, remember that you're on the edge of your dream world and that it's closer than it's ever been before.

Embrace the power of dream magic, and there'll be no end to what you can create.

Dream on, traveler.

Notes

Thank you for taking the time to read *Lucid Traveler*.

This work is always growing.
Expansion is the way forward.

If you have stories, comments, techniques, tips, or anything
useful and relevant to make lucid dreaming more accessible, please
contact:

Hello@AshlynLance.com

Alternatively, you can help spread this knowledge
by leaving reviews and recommending this book.
More interest, more dreamers!